Country File
Australia

Dana M. Rau

FRANKLIN WATTS
LONDON·SYDNEY

Revised and updated 2006

Franklin Watts
338 Euston Road, London
NW1 3BH

Franklin Watts Australia
Hachette Children's Books
Level 17/207 Kent Street
Sydney NSW 2000

COUNTRY FILE: AUSTRALIA produced for Franklin Watts by Bender Richardson White, PO Box 266, Uxbridge, UK.
Project Editor: Lionel Bender
Text Editors: Peter Harrison, Clare Oliver
Designer: Ben White
Picture Researcher: Cathy Stastny
Media Conversion and Make-up: Mike Pilley, Radius
Production: Kim Richardson

Graphics: Mike Pilley, Radius
Maps: Stefan Chabluk

For Franklin Watts:
Series Editor: Adrian Cole
Art Director: Jonathan Hair

A CIP catalogue record for this book is available from the British Library.

ISBN 0 7496 6631 5

Dewey Classification: 919.4

Printed in China

Picture Credits

Pages: 1: Corbis Images Inc. 3: Corbis Images Inc. 4: Hutchison Photo Library/Nick Haslam. 5-6: Corbis Images Inc. 7: Corbis Images Inc. 8: Corbis Images Inc. 9: Corbis Images Inc./Paul A. Souders. 10:Corbis Images Inc./ Richard Glover. 10–11 bottom: Corbis Images Inc. 12: Corbis Images Inc. 13: Corbis Images Inc.15: Corbis Images Inc. 16: Corbis Images Inc. 17: Corbis Images Inc.18: Corbis Images Inc./ Howard Davies. 19: David Simson. 20: Corbis Images Inc. 21: Corbis Images Inc. 22-23 bottom: Corbis Images Inc./ Robert Garvey. 23:Veronica Strang. Lampeter University. 24: Corbis Images Inc. 25: Hutchison Photo Library/ R. Ian Lloyd. 26-27: Eye Ubiquitous/ Adina Tovy Amsel. 29: Corbis Images Inc. 30: Corbis Images Inc. 31: Corbis Images Inc. Cover photo: Corbis Images Inc.

Note to parents and teachers

Every effort has been made by the Publishers to ensure that the websites in this book are suitable for children, that they are of the highest educational value, and that they contain no inappropriate or offensive material. However, because of the nature of the Internet, it is impossible to guarantee that the contents of these sites will not be altered. We strongly advise that Internet access is supervised by a responsible adult.

The Author

Dana M. Rau is a full-time writer and editor of non-fiction books. She has written more than 10 books for children about countries of the world.

Contents

Welcome to Australia

Australia is the largest island in the world. It is surrounded by the Indian Ocean to the west and the South Pacific Ocean to the east. It is located in an area of the world called Oceania.

Australia is unique because it is a single country but also a continent. Australia lies below the Equator in the southern hemisphere. This means that its seasons are opposite from those in northern countries: winter is from June to August, and summer from December to February.

A land of contrast

Australia has large, modern, bustling cities along its coast. By contrast the countryside, called 'the Outback', is mostly empty, flat and quiet. Some Australians, including those from Europe and Asia, are recent immigrants from other countries, while others, such as the Aborigines, have ancestors who have lived there for thousands of years.

The Melbourne skyline is peppered with skyscrapers – and new ones are being built all the time. ▼ ▼

INDONESIA

PAPUA NEW GUINEA

0°

5°S

10°S

15°S

20°S

25°S

30°S

35°S

40°S

45°S

50°S

INDIAN OCEAN

TIMOR SEA

CORAL SEA

Darwin

Gulf of Carpentaria

Great Barrier Reef

Broome

GREAT DIVIDING RANGE

Mitchell

Cairns

Townsville

Proserpine

Great Sandy Desert

NORTHERN TERRITORY

QUEENSLAND

Dampier

Flinders

Georgina

Rockhampton

Tropic of Capricorn

Ashburton

MACDONNELL RANGES

Alice Springs

Diamantina

Thomson

Uluru (Ayers Rock) △

Simpson Desert

Murchison

WESTERN AUSTRALIA

MUSGRAVE RANGES

SOUTH AUSTRALIA

Finke

Warrego

Brisbane

Laverton

Great Victoria Desert

L. Eyre

Culgoa

Geraldton

NEW SOUTH WALES

Darling

Newcastle

Perth

Great Australian Bight

Lachlan

Sydney

Bunbury

Adelaide

Mildura

CANBERRA

AUSTRALIAN CAPITAL TERRITORY

Albany

Port Lincoln

VICTORIA

Murray

GREAT DIVIDING RANGE

SOUTHERN OCEAN

Mt. Kosciuszko

Melbourne

Mount Gambier

TASMAN SEA

Bass Strait

Davenport

TASMANIA

Hobart

AUSTRALIA

Desert

Mountains

Grassland and farming

☐ Capital   ◯ Major city

Country boundary

State boundary

0   750 Miles

0   1000 Kilometres

N
W   E
S

105°E 110°E 115°E 120°E 125°E 130°E 135°E 140°E 145°E 150°E E

The Land

Australia is divided into three distinct regions: the Eastern Highlands, the Central Lowlands and the Great Western Plateau. The climate in the north is tropical because it benefits from summer rain and is close to the Equator. The middle of Australia is mostly sub-tropical, while the rest of the country is in the temperate zone.

The Eastern Highlands run from Australia's northern-most point, Cape York, down the eastern coast and into Tasmania. The Highlands are dominated by the Great Dividing Range, a string of hills and plateaus covered in grassland and forest. In the south-east, the mountains become higher and are known as the Australian Alps.

The Central Lowlands cover mid-eastern Australia. This region is very flat, with little rainfall and only tough grasses and shrubs survive. The land is suitable for raising sheep and cattle, but is of no use for growing crops.

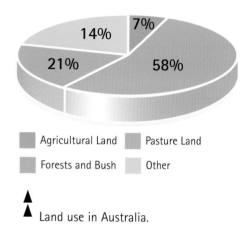

7%
14%
21%
58%

- Agricultural Land
- Pasture Land
- Forests and Bush
- Other

▲ Land use in Australia.

This forest of eucalyptus trees, palms and tree ferns is in Victoria, in south-eastern Australia. ▼

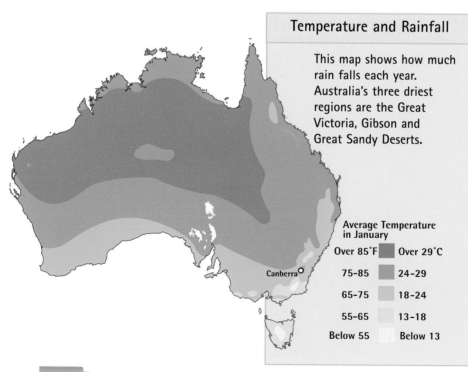

Temperature and Rainfall

This map shows how much rain falls each year. Australia's three driest regions are the Great Victoria, Gibson and Great Sandy Deserts.

Canberra○

Average Temperature in January	
Over 85°F	Over 29°C
75–85	24–29
65–75	18–24
55–65	13–18
Below 55	Below 13

Deserts, brush-fires and forests

The Great Western Plateau is a large, level area of raised land that covers about two-thirds of the continent. This remote part of the country is called the Bush or the Outback. The Plateau is covered by very dry deserts. Ancient rock formations dot the landscape, such as Uluru (Ayers Rock), the world's largest monolith standing at 330m (1,100ft).

Australia is one of the driest continents. Most of the hot, flat expanses of Australia receive very little rainfall. This sometimes causes brush-fires in the summer. Most rain falls along the coast, where more people live and work than elsewhere in Australia. The rain allows tropical forests to grow in the north, and temperate forests to grow in the south.

▶▶ A red kangaroo.

The summer and winter temperatures in five different cities. ▼

°C
40°

■ Range of average temperature

35°
Jan

30°
Jan July

25°
Jan

20°
July
Jan

15°
July

10°
July

5°

0°

Alice Springs   Darwin   Hobart   Perth   Sydney

°F
104°
95°
86°
77°
68°
59°
50°
41°
32°

Web Search ▶▶

▶ **www.gbrmpa.gov.au**
The Great Barrier Reef Marine Park Authority.

▶ **www.bom.gov.au**
Australian weather and climate.

▶ **www.ga.gov.au**
Maps of Australia (including some interactive ones).

The People

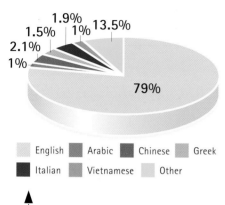

1.9%
1.5% 1% 13.5%
2.1%
1%

79%

- English
- Arabic
- Chinese
- Greek
- Italian
- Vietnamese
- Other

▲ English is the most widely used language, but there are also around 300 native languages.

```
        0      25      50      75 yrs
Male    ████████████████████ 77.5
Female  ██████████████████████ 83.4
```

▲ Life expectancy for men and women.

0.4% 0.6%
7%

92%

- Caucasian
- Asian
- Aboriginal
- Other

▲ Ethnic mix of the population.

►► An Aboriginal hunter near Darwin, in the Northern Territory. He is armed with traditional weapons, including a spear and boomerang.

Australians come from a rich mix of backgrounds. They live together in a way that is tolerant of their differences, although it was not always like this. Native Australians have had to fight for equality.

The first people living in Australia were the Aboriginal peoples and Torres Strait Islanders. The Torres Strait Islanders came from Melanesia and settled in Australia's northern islands about 10,000 years ago.

Ancient customs and traditions

The Aborigines walked over land bridges or travelled in boats to mainland Australia about 40,000 years ago from Asia. They settled into over 500 groups. The Aborigines hunted with spears and boomerangs and gathered food from the land. People all over the world have learned a lot about Aboriginal history and beliefs from their cave and rock paintings, which are scattered across Australia.

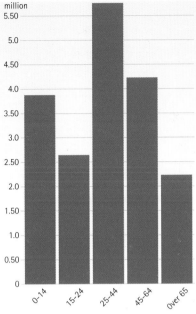

Age profile of the Australian population.

◄◄ Children of different ethnic backgrounds play at an outdoor party in the opal mining town of Coober Pedy in South Australia.

Settlers and immigrants

In 1788, British settlers created the first colonies in Australia. During the 1800s and early 1900s, immigrants came mainly from Britain or Ireland to farm or raise sheep. Some were criminals, shipped to ease overcrowding in British prisons. In the 1850s, many people from China arrived in Australia too, to work in gold mines.

In the second half of the 20th century, immigrants arrived from all over Europe and, by the 1970s, from Asia. Since World War II, more than five million people have moved to Australia from more than 150 countries.

Today, fewer than 3 per cent of the Australian population call themselves Aborigines or Torres Strait Islanders. Most of these people live in the cities and towns, but a few still live in the Outback and practise their ancestors' traditions.

Web Search ►►

► www.immi.gov.au
Details of immigration and multicultural affairs.

► www.atsic.gov.au
www.aiatsis.gov.au
Information about Aboriginals and Torres Strait Islanders.

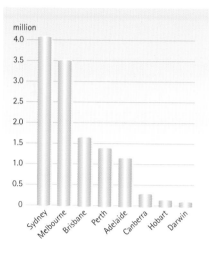

The number of people living in Australia's major cities.

This house in the suburbs of Brisbane is built of bricks and wood, with a tiled roof. Its design is similar to the style of houses built by the first British settlers in Australia in the early-1800s

A long straight stretch of road in central Australia, typical of highways in the Outback. ▼

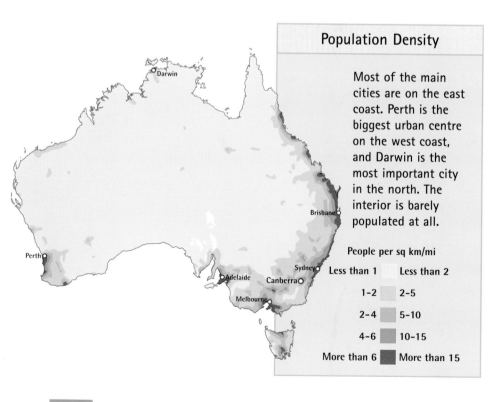

Population Density

Most of the main cities are on the east coast. Perth is the biggest urban centre on the west coast, and Darwin is the most important city in the north. The interior is barely populated at all.

People per sq km/mi

Less than 1	Less than 2
1-2	2-5
2-4	5-10
4-6	10-15
More than 6	More than 15

Urban and Rural Life

The south-eastern corner of the country, where city life is common, is home to the greatest number of Australians. More than 85 per cent of the entire population live and work there.

Australia's largest cities are its state and territory capitals. Sydney is the most populated and one of the largest commercial and financial centres in Australia. It is also one of the most important ports in the South Pacific Ocean. Melbourne, the second-largest city, is another important commercial centre. Together, the inhabitants of Sydney and Melbourne make up more than one-third of Australia's population.

Web Search ▶▶

▶ **www.cityofsydney.nsw. gov.au**
Sydney's official website.

▶ **www.act.gov.au**
Australian Capital Territory official website.

▶ **www.flyingdoctor.net**
The Royal Flying Doctor Service.

Suburban homes and rural properties

Australian cities are filled with tall skyscrapers, but most people in the city do not live in blocks of flats. They own single storey family houses in the suburbs that surround the city. These houses have gardens and verandas where people can relax in the evening after work.

Life in rural Australia is very different. Rural land takes up about 80 per cent of Australia, but only about 4 per cent of the population live there. The inhabitants are mostly farmers, property owners or miners.

Many properties are so big that people need to drive to see their neighbours. Properties are generally far from towns, too. A rural family may visit the nearest town for supplies once a week, or even more rarely. Their houses are usually large, with enough space for the family to live, plus an office for conducting property business, and plenty of outbuildings for storage. Weather in the Outback can be dangerously hot, and there is a lot of physical work to do. People can cool off in the local river or billabong.

Farming and Fishing

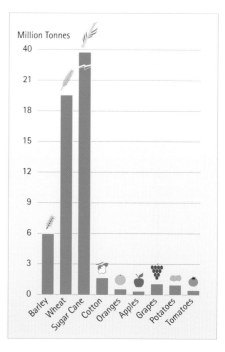

Australia has huge areas of land to exploit for farming. It is also completely surrounded by sea, which gives a lot of opportunity for commercial fishing. The fishing industry employs far fewer people than the farming industry, but it is expanding.

Sixty per cent of Australia's land is used for some type of farming or grazing. Most land is used for cattle and sheep grazing. In many parts of Australia, it is difficult for crops to grow because of flooding and droughts.

Australia's main export is wool, taken from the country's 98 million or more sheep. Cattle stations are based mostly in the northern and central parts of the Outback. They produce cattle for beef, another key export. Dairy products include butter, cheese and yoghurt. Poultry are another important source of income, with around 440 million chickens sold for meat each year.

Yearly production of the main arable crops.

Agricultural products

The main crops are sugar cane, wheat and barley. Farmers also grow rice, oats, cotton, and vegetables such as carrots, potatoes and tomatoes. Most arable farms are in the Eastern Highlands, where the land is most fertile.

Among the main fruits grown are oranges, pineapples and grapes and, in Tasmania, apples. Increasingly, grapes are made into fine Australian wines, which are exported around the world.

►► Australian farmers harvest over 6 million tonnes of barley a year, and 20 million tonnes of wheat. This wheat farm is in Western Australia.

The fishing industry

Australian offshore fishermen catch large quantities of black and blue marlin, tuna, and other smaller fish. They also catch prawns, lobsters and oysters. These shellfish are eaten by Australians and also exported, mostly to Japan.

Australians have begun some fish- (and reptile-) farming programmes. Instead of catching creatures from the wild, they raise oysters, prawns and even crocodiles in artificial lakes and ponds.

◄◄ Sheep are sheared once a year. The merino is the most popular breed. It produces beautifully soft, fine wool.

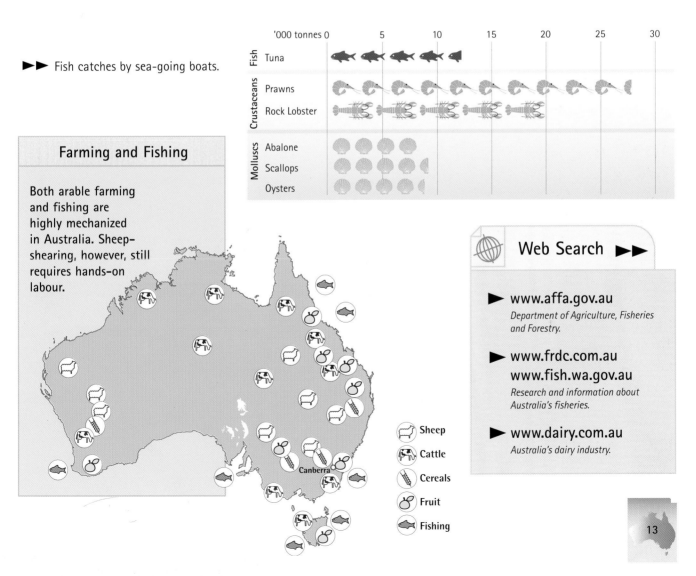

►► Fish catches by sea-going boats.

'000 tonnes	0	5	10	15	20	25	30

Fish
Tuna

Crustaceans
Prawns
Rock Lobster

Molluscs
Abalone
Scallops
Oysters

Farming and Fishing

Both arable farming and fishing are highly mechanized in Australia. Sheep-shearing, however, still requires hands-on labour.

Canberra

- 🐑 Sheep
- 🐂 Cattle
- 🌾 Cereals
- 🍎 Fruit
- 🐟 Fishing

🌐 Web Search ►►

► **www.affa.gov.au**
Department of Agriculture, Fisheries and Forestry.

► **www.frdc.com.au**
www.fish.wa.gov.au
Research and information about Australia's fisheries.

► **www.dairy.com.au**
Australia's dairy industry.

Resources and Industry

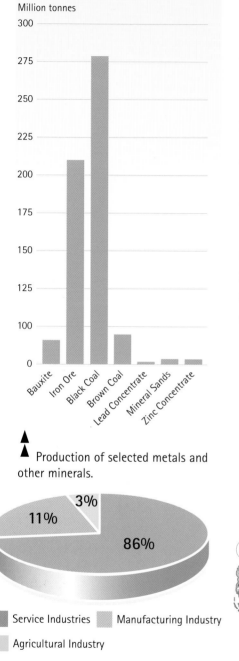

Million tonnes

▲ Production of selected metals and other minerals.

Service Industries ■ **Manufacturing Industry**
Agricultural Industry

3%
11%
86%

▲ The jobs that people do. The service sector is the largest employer.

Australia is rich in natural resources, especially minerals. These are mined and treated to produce materials that are useful both to Australians and to other people around the world. Although a wide range of goods are manufactured, this only employs a small number of Australians.

There are iron mines in the Pilbara region north of Perth and most bauxite and coal comes from Queensland. Coal, lead and zinc come from New South Wales and Victoria in the south produces oil and gas.

The other metals mined in Australia include silver, copper, nickel, tin, tungsten, uranium, manganese and, most precious of all, gold. Australians mine precious and semi-precious stones, too, such as opals, diamonds, pearls and sapphires.

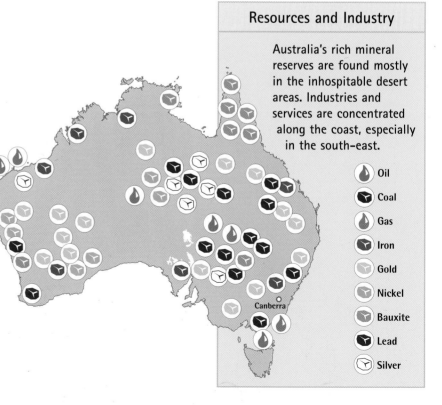

Resources and Industry

Australia's rich mineral reserves are found mostly in the inhospitable desert areas. Industries and services are concentrated along the coast, especially in the south-east.

- 🛢 Oil
- ⬢ Coal
- 🛢 Gas
- ⬢ Iron
- ◉ Gold
- ⬢ Nickel
- ⬢ Bauxite
- ⬢ Lead
- ⬢ Silver

Canberra

Manufacturing and the service industry

Australia is one of the world's largest producers of processed foods, including meat and dairy products, as well as animal feed. Other manufacturing industries include chemicals, plastics, electronics, paper and steel. Manufactured metal items include heavy machinery, transport equipment, appliances, small aircraft and motor vehicles. Most manufacturing takes place in Victoria and New South Wales.

The majority of Australia's workforce is employed in the service industry. This includes all jobs that provide a service to others, such as teaching in a school, or working in a bank, shop, hotel or restaurant. It also includes all of the workers involved in national or local government.

DATABASE

Energy Resources

Australia has natural reserves of coal, petroleum and natural gas which are used as fuel, but also imports crude oil from abroad. Most of the country's electricity is produced by coal-fired power stations. Australia's rich reserves of coal help keep the cost of electricity down.

In some homes, especially in remote areas, people are beginning to experiment with the use of alternative energy sources, such as solar power.

◄◄ An iron ore mine in the Hamersley Range. More than 90 per cent of Australia's iron ore comes from this highland region of north-west Western Australia.

Web Search ►►

► www.isr.gov.au
www.dewrsb.gov.au
Government departments for industry and employment.

► www.minerals.org.au
www.mininghall.com/minerals
Information from the Mineral Council of Australia and the Mining Hall of Fame.

► www.sacentral.sa.gov.au
Select the 'Business and Industry' directory to find out about South Central Australia's primary industries.

► www.abs.gov.au
Australian Bureau of Statistics, including labour force statistics.

Transport

Distances between places can be so great in Australia that an efficient transport system is essential. Road travel is now very popular, but the extensive railway network provides an alternative, both for personal and business transport.

Although Australia is a large country, it is very easy to travel around. There are nearly a million kilometres of roads and the National Highway connects all of the major cities. In total, there are over 13.2 million registered motor vehicles in Australia.

Trains on rails and roads

Railways also cross the continent and are found in each state, except Tasmania. Thousands of kilometres of track were laid in the 19th century when growing industries needed to move their products to the coast for export. The Trans-Australian Railway hauls freight to sea ports to this day. Australia's trains also carry nearly 600 million passengers a year. Not all are commuters; some people take trips on luxury trains as holidays. The Indian-Pacific Railway crosses the whole country, from Sydney to Perth. It boasts the record-breaking 'Long Straight', a 478-kilometre stretch of absolutely straight track between Ooldea and Nurin.

Large trucks, called road trains, pull heavy cargoes across the Outback day and night. They carry goods to the country's ports, to be shipped to other countries.

It is easy to see how road trains got their name. They pull trailers, as engines pull railway carriages. ▼

Boats and planes

Australia is an island and it can only be reached or left by plane or by boat. Australia's main ports include Sydney, Melbourne, Cairns, Brisbane, Adelaide, Fremantle and Geelong.

There are more than 400 airports in Australia, but most handle only internal flights. Sydney Airport is the busiest international airport, with almost seven million people passing through it each year.

This Boeing 747 is painted in the 'kangaroo' livery of Qantas, Australia's international airline.

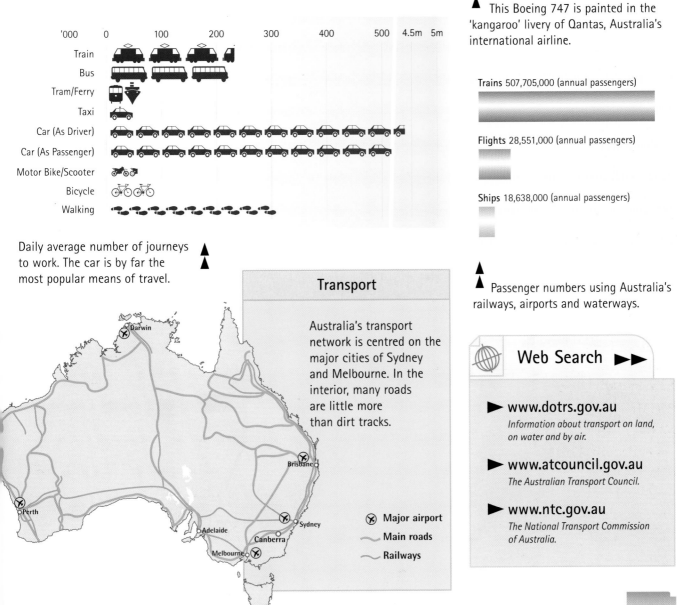

'000	0	100	200	300	400	500	4.5m	5m
Train								
Bus								
Tram/Ferry								
Taxi								
Car (As Driver)								
Car (As Passenger)								
Motor Bike/Scooter								
Bicycle								
Walking								

Daily average number of journeys to work. The car is by far the most popular means of travel.

Trains 507,705,000 (annual passengers)

Flights 28,551,000 (annual passengers)

Ships 18,638,000 (annual passengers)

Passenger numbers using Australia's railways, airports and waterways.

Transport

Australia's transport network is centred on the major cities of Sydney and Melbourne. In the interior, many roads are little more than dirt tracks.

Major airport
Main roads
Railways

Darwin
Perth
Brisbane
Adelaide
Sydney
Canberra
Melbourne

# Education

For Australians, the school year starts in January or early February and ends in December. There are plenty of schools for children to attend in towns and cities. In the Outback, where there may not be a town for hundreds of kilometres. Schools of the Air provide an alternative way for children to learn.

Some Australian children attend kindergarten from the age of five. All children must go to school from age six to age 15 or 16. Primary and secondary education are free, although some children go to private fee-paying schools.

The school day

During a normal day at school, children start class at 9 a.m. and take a short break during the morning. Lunch lasts for an hour, starting at 12.30 p.m. School ends around 3.30 p.m. After school, children go home to study or practise sports.

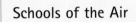
Schools of the Air

The Schools of the Air programme was set up in 1950 for children living in remote parts of the country. Students tune in to a two-way radio to talk with a teacher. The service has been improved with new satellite and Internet technology.

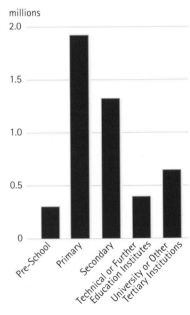

The number of pupils in schools at all levels.

◄◄ These university students in Melbourne are studying the geography of Australia.

School and beyond

Children attend primary school from age six. After Year 6 or 7 of primary school, they enter secondary school, where they stay until Year 10, when they are 15 or 16. Children study science, Australian history, mathematics, English, music and art. Some also take foreign languages.

At 15 or 16 students are free to leave and go to work, or to a college that will train them for a job. Many choose to stay for Year 11 and 12 instead. After this they can go on to study at a university. The University of Sydney and the University of Melbourne are Australia's oldest. Today, Australia has more than 30 colleges and universities.

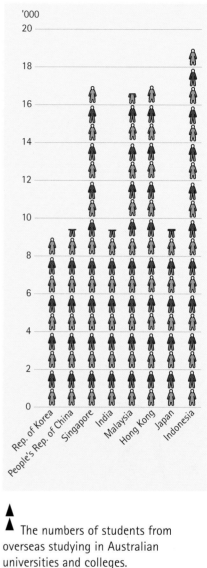

The numbers of students from overseas studying in Australian universities and colleges.

Most schoolchildren have the opportunity to visit galleries and museums as part of organized school outings.

Web Search ▶▶

▶ **www.detya.gov.au**
Commonwealth Department of Education, Training and Youth Affairs.

▶ **www.eddept.wa.edu.au**
www.edna.edu.au
Department of Education for Western Australia, and the Education Network Australia website.

Sport and Leisure

The climate allows Australians to take part in a wide variety of outdoor sports. There are approximately 6.5 million registered players of organized sports.

Children play such games as netball, cricket, tennis, gymnastics, soccer, rugby league, rugby union, Australian Rules football and hockey. Each year at local schools, children come together for a day of competition. Winners go on to compete in state and national championships. Most children in Australia have the opportunity to learn how to swim.

From swimming to netball

On the coasts, swimming, surfing, scuba diving, surfboat racing, sailing and fishing are popular. Elsewhere, pastimes include hiking, bicycling, horseback riding, tennis, polo and golf. Netball is the most popular sport among women.

In summer, cricket is the most watched professional sport. Football, rugby and Australian Rules Football – a mix of soccer and rugby – are played in winter.

Baseball and basketball are becoming increasingly popular. Horse-racing is popular, too, and all of Australia stops yearly on the first Tuesday of November to watch the Melbourne Cup horse race.

▶▶ Sailing in Whitsunday Passage, near the Great Barrier Reef.

Australian Rules Football

Australian Rules Football is one of the most popular games in Australia. 'Aussie Rules' is a rough and active game. It was first played in 1858. In September each year, more than 100,000 people gather to watch the Aussie Rules Grand Final game held in Melbourne.

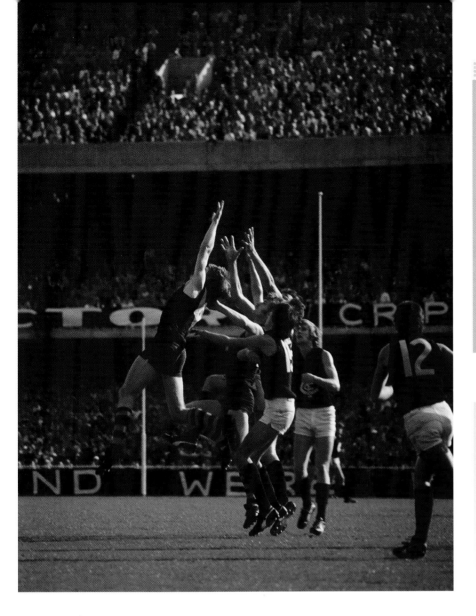

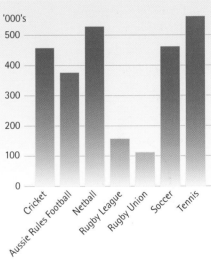

DATABASE

Sports Organizations

The Australian Sports Commission (ASC) is the government body in charge of sporting activities. More than one-third of Australians play sports and there are more than 30,000 local sporting clubs. About two-thirds of Australian children join a sporting club by the time they are 11 years old. These local clubs join with state clubs to form more than 100 national sporting organizations.

▲
Play is fast and furious during a game of Australian Rules football.

►► Sports club membership figures.

Olympic spirit

In 2000, Sydney hosted the 27th Summer Olympiad. Stadium Australia was built in the city as a venue for ceremonies and some of the competitions. Sydney also hosted the 11th Paralympiad for disabled athletes the same year. Australians were proud to be chosen to host the Olympics in such a momentous year, and to be recognized for their long sporting tradition.

🌐 **Web Search** ►►

► **www.australia.com**
The Australian Tourist Commission.

► **www.cricket.com.au**
Information from Cricket Australia.

► **www.afl.com.au**
Details of Australian Rules Football.

Daily Life and Religion

In Australia a family normally wakes up at around 7 a.m. Children go to school from 9 a.m. to 3.30 p.m., and adults go to work from 9 a.m. to 5 p.m.

Children have their own organized activities after school. Some go to sporting clubs. Many children belong to Boy Scouts or Girl Guides. In the Outback, children typically have to do jobs around the house or property after they finish their schoolwork.

On weekends, families might go to a national park or visit a shopping centre, or 'mall.' Australians living near the coast also spend a lot of the time at the beach. When the weather is fine, Australians often have a 'barbie' (barbecue) outdoors where meat or seafood is grilled over hot charcoal.

The Royal Flying Doctor Service

If someone falls ill in the Outback, the nearest doctor's surgery may be hundreds of kilometres away. The Royal Flying Doctor Service (RFDS) sends medical staff out in planes to patients in remote areas. Most patients can be treated on the spot; some are flown to the nearest hospital.

Looking after the nation

The Australian Defence Force (ADF) is made up of the Army (about 25,500 full-time staff), Navy (13,100) and Air Force (13,500). Australian citizens and permanent residents only can join at age 17.

Australia has a public national healthcare system that is funded through taxes and 'Medicare' contributions paid by all taxpayers. Medicare pays 85% of medical fees or 100% in the case of children and the elderly.

Ownership of cars, telephones and TVs for every 1,000 people in the population. ▼▼

	0	100	200	300	400	500	600	700	800	900	1000
Motor Vehicles											
Telephones											
Mobile Phones											
Televisions											

Families relaxing on the beach in Perth. Swimming, surfing, shopping and sightseeing are favourite leisure pursuits. ▼

1.4% 1.9% 1.2%
23.5% 20%
28%
17% 7%

Islam ■ Buddhism ■ Other Non-Christian
Anglican Catholic Uniting Church
Other Christian Not Registered

▲ The numbers of Australians practising major religions.

Web Search ▶▶

▶ www.aihw.gov.au
The Australian Institute of Health and Welfare.

▶ www.catholic.org.au
The Catholic Church in Australia.

▶ www.defence.gov.au
The Department of Defence.

▲ Aboriginal rock art. Aboriginal paintings often depict Dreamtime.

Religion

Traditional Aboriginal beliefs centre on the spirit world. The most important stories are about 'Dreamtime'. This is the Aboriginal explanation of Creation, the time when spirits created the land and made it good for humans.

The primary religion among most of the population is Christianity. Australians come from many parts of the world, however, and other religions, including Islam, Buddhism and Judaism, are also practised.

Arts and Media

The complex mix of peoples in Australia has produced a lively arts scene. There is also an amazing choice of newspapers and magazines, radio stations and television channels.

The government helps fund many arts programmes, including the national Australian Ballet and Opera Australia. All of the state capitals have art museums, their own orchestra, opera and theatre. The National Gallery of Australia is in Canberra.

Aboriginal art

The Aboriginal peoples have a flourishing artistic culture. At corroborees, they gather to dance and play music. The didgeridoo is a traditional instrument. Aboriginal paintings depict people, animals and mythical creatures on bark, cave walls or wood. Today, Aboriginal artwork can be as easily found on the Internet. New virtual galleries showcase the latest work.

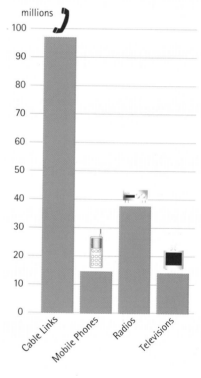

Total numbers of phones and other communications media owned by businesses and people in Australia.

◄◄ The Sydney Opera House, the landmark arts venue that was completed in 1973.

24

Shoppers are entertained at an arcade in Cairns, Queensland. Australia has a unique mix of people from many different cultures.

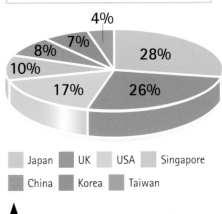

4%
7%
8%
10%
28%
17%
26%

Japan   UK   USA   Singapore
China   Korea   Taiwan

Numbers of tourists visiting Australia each year.

The media and broadcasting

More than 1,200 magazines and dozens of newspapers are published in Australia, including the *Sydney Morning Herald*. The *Australian*, established in 1964, is the country's only national daily newspaper.

The Government runs the Australian Broadcasting Corporation (ABC), which provides radio and television without commercials. There are also a number of commercial radio and television stations. Multicultural programming is serviced by the Special Broadcasting Service (SBS).

Tourism

More than four million people visit Australia each year, making tourism one of the country's fastest-growing industries. They come from all over the world, especially from Japan, Great Britain and the United States. They relax on the beautiful beaches, visit historical sites and buildings, trek through the rainforest and snorkel along the Great Barrier Reef.

Government

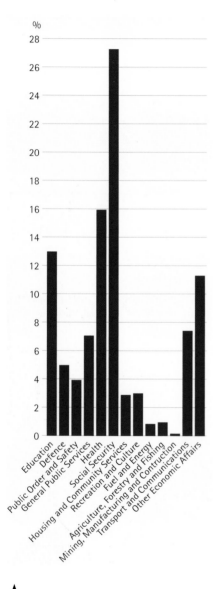

%
28
26
24
22
20
18
16
14
12
10
8
6
4
2
0

Education
Defence
Public Order and Safety
General Public Services
Health
Social Security
Housing and Community Services
Recreation and Culture
Fuel and Energy
Agriculture, Forestry and Fishing
Mining, Manufacturing and Contruction
Transport and Communications
Other Economic Affairs

Government spending on different sectors, as a percentage of the total.

Australia is a parliamentary democracy that is modelled on the government of Great Britain. However, unlike Great Britain, Australia has a written Constitution. Australia was once a British colony but became an independent nation in 1901.

Australia still holds traditional ties to Britain. The head of state in Australia is Queen Elizabeth II. While she does not actually rule in Australia, the Queen appoints a governor-general to represent her.

Parliament

Australia's Parliament is made up of the House of Representatives and the Senate. Members of Parliament are elected by the people. To be able to vote, people must be 18 or over. In Australia it is compulsory to vote and people are fined if they do not. More than 90 per cent of Australians vote.

The House of Representatives and the Senate meet ▼ here, at the Parliament Building in Canberra. ▼

This map shows the six states and two territories that make up Australia. Each has its own government and local councils.

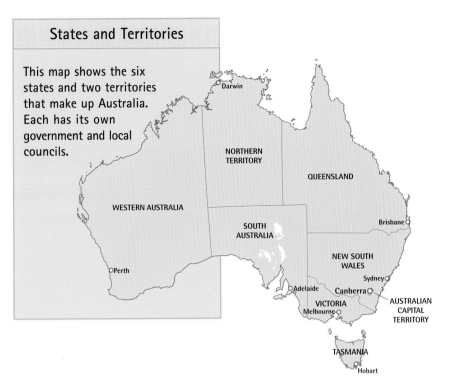

Darwin

NORTHERN TERRITORY

QUEENSLAND

WESTERN AUSTRALIA

Brisbane

SOUTH AUSTRALIA

NEW SOUTH WALES

Perth

Sydney

Adelaide

Canberra

VICTORIA

Melbourne

AUSTRALIAN CAPITAL TERRITORY

TASMANIA

Hobart

Who Governs What?

The Government is in charge of defence, income taxes and immigration policy.

The state and territorial governments are in charge of education, transport, healthcare and the police.

Local councils are in charge of maintaining towns, roads and waste disposal. They also provide facilities, including sports centres and libraries.

Running the country, states and territories

The House of Representatives makes the laws, which then need to be passed by a majority in the Senate. Members of the House and Senate belong to political parties.

Whichever party has a majority in the House of Representatives runs the Government and the leader of the majority party becomes the Prime Minister. He or she selects Parliament members to make up the Cabinet. Usually they are from his or her own party. With the Cabinet's help, the Prime Minister makes important decisions.

States and territories have their own governments and courts. Premiers act as the leaders of the states and Chief Ministers are leaders of the territories.

DATABASE

How Parliament is Organized

The House of Representatives has 148 seats. Representatives are elected from the six states and two territories. They are elected for a maximum term of three years.

The Senate has 76 seats. Each state elects 12 Senators, and each territory elects two. State senators sit for 6-year terms.

Web Search ►►

► www.australia.gov.au
The Australian Government website.

► www.aph.gov.au
The Australian Parliament's website.

► www.pm.gov.au
The prime minister's official website.

► www.aec.gov.au
The Australian Electoral Commission, which organizes Australian elections.

Place in the World

Australia's size and geographical position mean it occupies a crucial place in the development of South-east Asia and in global politics and economics. It is a member of the Asian Pacific Economic Cooperation (APEC), as well as the Association of South-east Asian Nations (ASEAN).

Australia's international aid program focuses on assisting developing Asian-Pacific countries. It aims to help them reduce poverty and achieve sustainable development.

Australia earns a great deal of money from its exports, most of which go to Japan. Among the main exports are farm products, minerals and other raw materials, and manufactured goods. Coal, beef, cotton, wheat and wool are also exported. The high demand for manufactured goods such as cars and computers is met by imports from the European Union (EU), the United States and Japan.

Australia has encouraged valuable foreign investment by removing many trade barriers. Foreign investment in Australia totals around A$904 billion each year and tourism today also generates a significant amount.

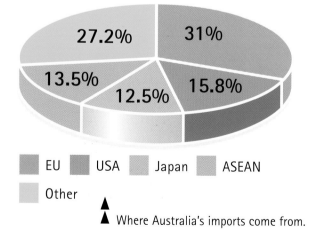

EU   USA   Japan   ASEAN   Other

▲ Where Australia's imports come from.

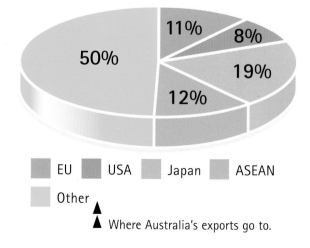

EU   USA   Japan   ASEAN   Other

▲ Where Australia's exports go to.

Major exports, in A$ billions. ▼▼

Billion A$

Coal	8.7
Non-Monetary Gold	5.7
Iron Ore	5.4
Aluminium	3.6
Wheat	3.4
Meat	5.7
Aluminium Ores	3.4
Wood	4.9
Crude Petroleum	4.5
Refined Petroleum	1.9

▲ The Great Barrier Reef is more than 2,200km long and is home to more than 10,000 different species.

Looking to the future

The influx of people from different countries has also helped to improve life for the indigenous population. After facing prejudice for many years, indigenous groups have finally been given the right to claim back land that was taken from them in the past by white settlers.

As Australia faces the future, its citizens have been discussing whether Australia should become a republic and break its remaining ties with Britain. When the issue was put to the Australian people late in 1999, 55 per cent voted against the country's becoming a republic, but the debate continues.

Web Search ▶▶

▶ www.dfat.gov.au
Department of Foreign Affairs and Trade.

▶ www.ausaid.gov.au
Australia's overseas aid programme.

▶ www.foundingdocs.gov.au
Tells the story of Australia and has links to real historical documents.

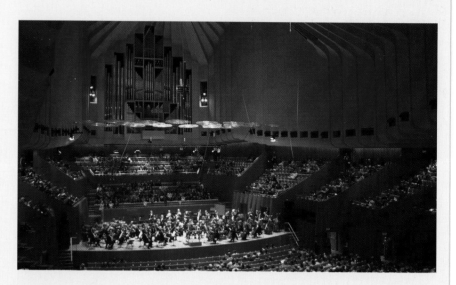

Area:
7,682,300 sq km

Population size:
20,111,297

Capital city:
Canberra (population 387,000)

Other major cities:
Sydney, Melbourne, Brisbane, Perth, Adelaide, Darwin and Hobart

Longest river:
Murray-Darling River system (3,370 km)

Highest mountain:
Mount Kosciuszko (2,229 m)

Flag:
The Australian flag has a background of blue, with the Union Jack of the United Kingdom in the upper left corner. Under it is a star called the Commonwealth Star which represents Australia. It has seven points, one for each state and one for both territories. The other half of the flag shows the constellation of the Southern Cross, made up of four seven-pointed stars and one five-pointed star. All of the stars are white.

National Anthem:
'Advance Australia Fair'

Official language:
English

Currency:
Australian dollar (A$)

Major resources:
Coal, iron, bauxite, lead, zinc, oil, gas, silver, copper, nickel, tin, tungsten, uranium and manganese

Major exports:
Aluminium, beef, coal, iron ore, bauxite, wheat, wool, machinery and transport equipment

National holidays and major events:
New Year's Day (1 January)
Australia Day (26 January)
Regatta Day, Tasmania (February)
Launceston Cup Day (February)
Sydney Mardi Gras (February or March)
Canberra Day (March)
Commonwealth Day (March)
Good Friday, Easter Saturday, Easter Day and Easter Monday (March or April)
ANZAC Day (25 April)
May Day (first Monday in May)
Mothers' Day (May)
Adelaide Cup Day (May)
Queen's Official Birthday (June)
Picnic Day, Northern Territory (August)
The Royal National Australia (RNA) Show, Brisbane (mid-August)
Fathers' Day (September)
Melbourne Cup Day (November)
Christmas Day (25 December)
Boxing Day (26 December)
Proclamation Day (26 December)

Religions:
Christianity (Roman Catholicism, Anglican, Uniting Church of Australia and others), Islam, Buddhism, Judaism, Hinduism, Sikhism, Baha'i, Aboriginal traditional beliefs, Chinese traditional beliefs

Glossary

AGRICULTURE
growing crops or raising animals.

ARABLE
land used for growing crops rather than raising livestock.

CLIMATE
the average weather conditions experienced in one area over a period of time.

COLONY
an area of land that is taken over, settled and ruled by another country.

COMMUTER
someone who makes the same journey to a particular place day after day.

CONSTITUTION
a written document that describes the responsibilities of a government.

CONTINENT
one of Earth's seven largest landmasses.

ECONOMY
the organization of a country's money and resources.

EQUATOR
an imaginary line around the globe that divides the northern and southern hemispheres.

ETHNIC
belonging to a particular race or culture.

EXPORTS
the goods and services a country sells to other countries.

FERTILE
land suitable for growing crops.

GOVERNMENT
the organization that sets and enforces laws for a nation.

IMMIGRANTS
people who move from one country to live in another.

IMPORTS
the goods and services a country buys from other countries.

MANUFACTURING
using machinery to make products from raw materials.

MULTICULTURALISM
the coming together of many different cultures and ways of life.

INDIGENOUS
belonging naturally to a place.

POPULATION
the number of people who live in a certain area.

RESOURCES
a country's supplies of energy, natural materials and minerals.

RURAL
relating to the countryside.

SERVICE INDUSTRIES
industries which provide a service to people rather than make products.

SUBURBS
areas of housing in towns and cities between the centre and the countryside.

URBAN
relating to towns and cities.

31

Index